SOUTH AFRICA IN BLACK AND WHITE

SOUTH AFRICA

IN BLACK AND WHITE

JUHAN KUUS

TEXT BY TREVOR McDONALD

HARRAP
London

First published in Great Britain 1987
by HARRAP Ltd

Illustrations © Juhan Kuus 1987
Introduction © Trevor McDonald 1987

ISBN 0 245-54543-3

Printed and bound in Great Britain
by R.J. Acford Ltd, Chichester, Sussex

When I despair, I remember that all through history the way of truth and love has always won.

There have been tyrants and murderers and for a time they can seem invincible, but in the end they always fall – think of it – always.

Mahatma Gandhi

Acknowledgements

This book is dedicated to all photographers who continue to work under repressive regimes and dangerous circumstances in their endeavours to record and tell the truth through their medium.

I wish to thank my parents, Jimmy Soullier, chief photographer of the Johannesburg *Sunday Times*, and his friend, Ian Berry, also Don Laught, Trevor Simon, Percy and Marie Dean, Phyllis Springer, Denise Goksin and all the SIPA staff in Paris.

I do not pretend to be a political expert on the problems facing South Africa today nor do I offer a solution. I prefer to see my role merely as a photographer recording what I see and experience. I neither support nor endorse any ideology whatsoever. Difficult as it may seem, I do not take sides — I take photographs. I am against all forms of violence. Violence perpetrated on the individual or on nations cannot be condoned.

Juhan Kuus, London, 1987

Introduction

My first visit to South Africa, in the autumn of 1984, coincided with what the Pretoria Government saw as a significant constitutional development.

The year before, the Government had published its Constitution Bill, which provided for the first time for the inclusion of 'Coloureds' and 'Indians' in a revised Parliamentary system.

In a three-chamber Parliament, there is today an 'Indian' chamber with 45 seats (The House of Delegates), a Coloured chamber with 85 seats (The House of Representatives), and a white chamber with 178 seats (The House of Assembly).

The three chambers elected members to an electoral college on the same 4:2:1 ratio, so that it comprised 50 whites, 25 'Coloureds' and 13 'Indians'. In September 1984 this college elected Mr P. W. Botha as executive President for a seven-year term with comprehensive powers to dictate the manner in which the affairs of Parliament should be run. For example, a President's council consisting of 60 members, 25 nominated by the President and the other 35 elected on a 4:2:1 ratio, can discuss matters as defined by the President as 'common to all racial groups'. Significantly, the separate 'Indian' and 'Coloured' chambers may only discuss what are referred to as 'own affairs'.

Not surprisingly, the birth and the aims of the tri-chamber legislature fell far short of the nationalist aspirations of non-white South Africans.

Black leaders felt that the new Constitution seemed to go out of its way to confirm the exclusion of 'Africans' from the politics of their country. Those who campaigned against the elections to the tri-chamber Parliament made much of the fact that in a country of 33 million people in which whites account for 18 per cent, 'Coloureds' for 9 per cent and 'Indians' for a miniscule 3 per cent, the Government had gone to extraordinary lengths to establish a minorities political league and to exclude 'Africans' or blacks, who account for no fewer than 70 per cent of the population.

In the campaign against elections for the three-chamber Parliament led by the broad-based umbrella group, the United Democratic Front, it was stated, and has since been frequently repeated, that the purpose of the 1983 Constitution Bill was to urge 'Coloureds' and 'Indians' 'to close ranks with whites in the extended laager and to make "Indians" and "Coloureds" responsible jointly with the minority whites, for the administration of the hated apartheid laws which operate against the country's overwhelming black majority'.

The United Democratic Front's campaign calling for a boycott of the elections to the new Parliament was widely viewed as a success. The percentage of 'Coloured' and 'Indian' voters was tiny. But the Government felt the plan was worth pursuing, a fact which confirmed black political leaders like the Reverend Allan Boesak, Archbishop Desmond Tutu and Chief Mangosuthu Gatsha Buthelezi that the Government was simply attempting to remodel the apartheid system to maintain the economic, social and political ascendancy of whites, with the resultant unequal sharing of wealth between the minority white population and other communities.

The new three-chamber Parliament has had its problems, most notable of which has been the threat by the leader of the 'Coloured' chamber that he will take his members out of the system unless the Government abandons one of the principal pillars of apartheid: The Group Areas Act, which dictates where people may live, and under which over the years hundreds of thousands of families have been 're-located'.

Of much greater interest to black political leaders has been what they see as the manner in which the 1983 Constitution Bill defines the Government's view about how far any future political 'reforms' will be allowed to go.

The limits of any plans for 'reform' were in fact clearly stated by the Minister for Constitutional Development in the Parliamentary debate on the 1983 Bill.

Minister Chris Heunis began by explaining that South African society was extremely complex and with what he called a 'higher tension potential' because of 'its great varieties and diversities'. He said that the 1983 Bill ensured greater sovereignty, the granting of self-determination and the recognition of the 'interests of minorities'. The aim of the Bill, he asserted, was to 'bring about reform in which each person and group would acquire an effective say in the decision-making process as they affected each group but without the values of that group being impaired'. The Minister acknowledged that African constitutional development was a high priority for his government, but emphasized that Africans had a separate constitutional path to follow. Mr Heunis rejected the concept of 'power sharing', admitting that the terms 'sharing of responsibilities' and 'division of power' were more appropriate.

The minority white Government in Pretoria has so far been unable to find an acceptable formula for that 'separate constitutional path' for black people to follow.

Since that debate, the Government of President Botha has instituted a series of reforms to the apartheid systems. But black leaders see Mr Heunis's statements as indicating this important bottom line: The minority white African Government has no intention of sharing power with the majority blacks. The provisions of the 1983 Bill are meant to ensure that whites will always remain in the ascendant and that 'non whites' will never constitutionally be allowed to challenge or to change that. As the official opposition, the Progressive Federal Party, said during the debate on the Constitutional Bill, its provisions fail to address 'the central question of black-white co-existence' and in that way retain one of the fundamental tenets of apartheid: the separation of the races. In the words of the Progressive Federal Party, the Constitution's distinction between 'own' and 'general' affairs, served to 'entrench apartheid' and the establishment of racially separate houses and racially separate ministers' councils 'reinforced racial separation and discrimination'.

So, right at the very moment of its most creative burst of political reform, the Government's provisions were seen as maintaining the status quo. And when the heads of six homeland administrations rejected the new Constitution, they did so because, in their words, it 'made racial divisions the guiding principles of the State and excluded 70 per cent of the population from the political process'.

The Government's Constitution Bill fared no better with the important South African business sector. Harry Oppenheimer, former Chairman of the Anglo-American Corporation, said that black people bitterly resented the introduction of measures without reference to their opinions, adding that 'further alienation of blacks was too high a price to pay for the advantages of Coloured and Indian representation in Parliament'. Dr Zach De Beer said the provisions insulted blacks by asking whites to turn their backs on them and swindled Coloured people and Indians by bringing them into a Parliamentary system in which they had no real power. Mr Tony Bloom, Chairman of the Premier Group, described the Constitution as 'a step in the wrong direction'.

Many newspapers also criticized the plan, calling it 'half baked and ill conceived', 'unworkable, undemocratic, and terribly foolish'.

The *Pretoria News* said that at best the Constitution was wholly inadequate, at worst a 'Machiavellian design to place the (governing) National Party permanently in the driving seat with a multi-racial collection of passengers for cosmetic effect'.

The real problem for the South African Government today is that after the 1983 Constitution, even when it attempts to remove some of the irritations of what is called 'petty apartheid', it is still dogged by the perception that it is a million miles away from important fundamental principles – like common citizenship and nationality, the right of all adults to have a voice in central political institutions, including Parliament; a judicially protected Bill of Rights and the elimination of racial discrimination.

This is the precise context in which the sanctions debate began and the context in which it must be viewed. Before the Pretoria Government announced its plans for a new Constitution in 1983, many black leaders were openly sceptical about whether there was the commitment in the National Party to institute genuine reform. The conspicuous exclusion of the majority black population from the 1983 provisions convinced blacks that their scepticism was justified. The view began to gain ground that those who controlled the system had no intention of changing it radically. Other means, it was argued, must be sought. And the argument for international sanctions, chief among them economic sanctions, became one of the centrepieces of the whole South African debate.

The South African Government argued strenuously against the strident calls of economic sanctions. The debate is by no means over, but the possibility looms that the South African Government may lose its case against sanctions.

Those who argue against sanctions emphasize the need for continuing to trade with South Africa if that country is not to be driven beleaguerd into the laager of international isolation and away from the acknowledgement that only with radical change can it ever hope to survive.

Those who canvass the case for sanctions argue that the desired radical change will only came about if the major Western governments take punitive action to show their disapproval of the status quo.

And there are a number of positions in between.

The advocates of economic sanctions point to the often repeated claim by the South Africans that blacks will be hardest hit. That, say the people who call for sanctions, is the clearest evidence of the duplicity of the Pretoria Government, who having ignored the call for black political rights, now suddenly feigns an interest in black economic well-being.

It is just possible, though, that the argument is becoming academic. The fact is that a growing number of countries have decided to distance themselves from South Africa. In the business sector nearly 90 firms and corporations, like the American giants EXXON, IBM and General Motors, have decided to dilute their ties with South Africa.

Perhaps one of the best summations of the sanctions argument comes from the Catholic Institute of International Relations. The publication in which this assessment is made, is banned in South Africa itself, rendering the chance for any full and informed debate difficult. But this is in effect what it says:

The international corporate community do perhaps cynically believe that it will be 'business as usual' after black majority rule and that their undeniable economic power will be the last word in deliberations about social justice and economic change. But there is no adequate historical justification for such a belief. At the 1985 Lusaka meeting it was the ANC (African National Congress), not the businessmen, who set out their plans for a future South Africa that involved fundamental changes. The future of South African black nationalism in the 1980s suggests a determination to gain power and transform socio-economic relations in the Republic and the capacity ultimately to do so. Whether this transformation takes place in a totalitarian state after massive bloodshed and the destruction of the region's economy in a war to last decades, depends in some measure on the West's capacity to perceive its strategic interests in the perspective of something more than short-term company profits. For the magnitude of the change likely to take place in South Africa should be measured against the upheaval of the Iranian revolution, rather than the relatively smooth transition in Zimbabwe. And the magnitude of the West's ignorance about the true political state of black communities in South Africa had striking parallels in both Zimbabwe and Iran during the 1970s. Given the mineral wealth of the Republic, the implications of such a change, and such a misunderstanding for the Western world, and for world peace, need no underlining.

It lies within the power of the West to shorten the disruptive transition to black majority rule in South Africa and, possibly, to save countless lives. To do so requires an act of political will and a prudent judgement of national interests. Effective economic sanctions imposed by the USA, Britain, West Germany, Japan and France hold out the hope of pre-empting a prolonged civil war and the devastation of the South African economy. The collapse of the Rand in 1985, after only two American banks refused to renew their loans to South Africa, demonstrated the economic power in the hands of the West. If the West fails to wield this power effectively, substituting rhetoric for decisive action, it will remain an accomplice in what follows.

The Commonwealth was the international forum in which the sanctions issue was most passionately debated. That is not surprising. The Commonwealth prides itself on its multi-racial nature, an association of nearly 50 independent countries embracing countless races and cultures in a largely harmonious and equal partnership—in the words of the Head of the Commonwealth, the Queen, 'an immense union of nations with their homes set in all four corners of the earth'. The Commonwealth evolved out of the old British Empire; and its principles as part of the new spirit of association in the fading twilight of Britain's imperial power.

Until 1961 South Africa was a member of what was then called the British Commonwealth of Nations. But in that year, following a row over its policy of apartheid, South Africa, faced with expulsion from the multi-racial body, decided to leave of its own accord.

Since that time, the question of South Africa has been discussed frequently at Commonwealth meetings; and at the Commonwealth Heads of Government meeting in Nassau in the Bahamas in 1985, it was decided after a long debate to send a group of eminent persons on a mission to the Republic to assess what the prospects were for a negotiated settlement between the white minority and the black majority.

Two points about this were important. The first was that the mission had been decided on because the Commonwealth had failed to reach a common position on the issue of sanctions; the mission was intended to advance the possibility of that. And the second factor was that the mission was undertaken at a time when the words 'political reforms' were on the lips of nearly every senior South African politician.

President B.W. Botha had led the way and in a series of major speeches he had boldly declared that in South Africa the status quo could no longer be maintained and that South Africa should adapt to changing times.

Although the Commonwealth Group modestly disclaimed the title of 'eminent persons', its participants were of some distinction. Malcolm Fraser, former Prime Minister of Australia, and General Olusegun Obasanjo were co-chairman. The British nominee was Lord Barber, former Chancellor of the Exchequer and chairman of Standard Chartered Bank, an institution with hugh South African interests. The rest of the group were representatives from India, Tanzania, a Barbadian representative of the World Council of Churches and a primate of the Anglican Church of Canada.

Although South Africa is probably one of the most thoroughly studied countries on earth, there has never been anything like the visit of the Commonwealth Eminent Persons Group. Its work and its findings carried special weight because its members were able to talk to South African Government ministers, allowed to visit the imprisoned black leader Nelson Mandela, and also allowed to travel around the country to listen to the views of other leaders in many other spheres of life in the Republic. And without ever having said so publicly, the Reagan administration, facing a rebellious Congress calling for tougher action against South Africa, was anxious to learn how the Eminent Persons Group would fare and to hear what its conclusions were.

When the history of this period comes to be written, it may well be recorded that the visit of the Commonwealth Group did a great deal to change international perceptions about South Africa.

The mission's conclusion was that 'despite appearances and statements to the contrary, the South African Government is not yet ready to negotiate...fundamental change, nor to countenance the creation of genuine democratic structures, nor to face the prospect of the end of white domination'. The report made this critical observation about the Government's programme of reform: 'Its programme of reform does not end apartheid, but seeks to give it a less inhuman face...' It went on:

'Behind these attitudes lies a deeper truth. After more than 18 months of persistent unrest, upheavals and killings unprecedented in the country's history [this was written in June 1986] the Government believes that it can contain the situation indefinitely by use of force.'

On the very day the report was published, President Botha imposed drastic emergency regulations to contain growing black unrest.

The Commonwealth report said that South African blacks who made up 70 per cent of their country's population would never give up their vision of equal humanity: 'They can no longer stomach being treated as aliens in their own country; to believe that they can be indefinitely suppressed is an act of self-delusion.' The Group's grim conclusion was that should the major Western nations find it impossible to convince the South Africans to negotiate a pragmatic and genuine power-sharing arrangement, 'the cost in lives may have to be counted in millions'.

On that question of the possibility of a 'negotiated settlement', it's probably useful to quote the Eminent Persons report again. This is what it says: 'In regard to the modalities of negotiation, the Government's position has a considerable element of wishful thinking. The Government is willing and ready to negotiate with "responsible" leaders; if only violence and intimidation would abate, these leaders would be ready to come to the negotiating table to strike a deal. Although we were never told by the Government who these responsible leaders might be, it could be inferred that prominent among them would be the "homelands" leaders whom the Government repeatedly urged us to see. With the exception of Chief Buthelezi, the "homeland" leaders have no real political standing or following and would not, in our view, be credible parties in a negotiation to resolve South Africa's deepening crisis.'

The Commonwealth Eminent Persons Group went further. Its members came to a firm view about the body with which the South African Government should negotiate.

Its report said: 'There can be no negotiated settlement in South Africa without the ANC; the breadth of its support is incontestable and this support is growing.' The South African Government does not share any of these views. And the Eminent Persons Group was only too well aware of that fact:

'The Government makes it clear that it does not regard the ANC as the only other party to negotiations.

We agree, but would emphasize that the ANC is a necessary party. The Government acknowledge this, if only by blaming the ANC for most of the violence.'

The Commonwealth Group visited the ANC leader Nelson Mandela who has been imprisoned for 24 years. Those who saw Mandela reported that they were struck by his physical authority, his immaculate appearance and by his commanding stature. His attitude to people outside the ANC was described as 'reasonable and conciliatory'. And Mr Mandela took care to emphasize his desire for reconcialition across the divide of colour. Mr Mandela described himself as a deeply committed South African nationalist, but he acknowledged, in his conversation with the Commonwealth Group, that nationalists come in more than one colour. He pledged himself anew to work for a multiracial society in which all would have a secure place...he recognized the fears of white people and emphasized the importance of minority groups being given a real sense of security in any new society in South Africa.

The view of the Commonwealth Eminent Persons Group was that Mandela should be released from prison.

Mandela told the Eminent Persons Group that once he was released he would tour the sprawling black townships in his country with his ANC colleagues, urging an end to violence and supporting negotiations.

And that is why, despite the failure of the Commonwealth Group to smooth the way to a negotiated settlement in South Africa, the glimmering hope for racial peace in the country can be prevented from fading away altogether.

And that is the view of many South Africans and foreign observers who believe that Mr Mandela is the only person who may be able to prevent a race war in his country. One of the strongest anti-apartheid voices in the country, Mrs Helen Suzman, says: 'Mandela is the last hope for a negotiated solution between blacks and whites.' Winnie Mandela also believes that the release of her husband affords South Africa its last chance. She says: 'His is the last generation of peaceful resistance. Among the younger generation, there is no room whatsoever for negotiations.'

Mrs Mandela also says this about the Government's attempt to bottle up rising black discontent and anger by its 'reforms':

'The black man does not have the word "reform" in his vocabulary. Blacks in this country are talking about the transition of power to the majority. The Government will not release Mandela because he will negotiate only a transfer of power. The Afrikaner is very far from accepting that.'

How easy or how difficult was it for me to report events in South Africa with impartiality? I think that has a great deal to do with the very strong tradition in British journalism always to present, as fairly as one is able, both sides of an argument. It's part of the great sense in this country of reporting in a manner which can be described as fair. And, as even the Government of South African admits, some things cry out so loudly for drastic change, that the principal job of a journalist becomes reporting the situation as he finds it, describing what he sees and trying to give his audience any information which he thinks might be relevant in explaining why things are as they are. That's the tradition of reporting in this country and instead of getting too involved, when such an involvement may prejudice what one says, it's so much better to present what you see, try to explain as best you can, and let people who watch what you do make up their own minds. That's what they end up doing in any event, and the very sophisticated television viewers in this country do not appreciate reports which are very obviously biased. In reporting in South Africa, I talked to Government ministers, to right-wing politicians, to people in the street, to lawyers and community workers, to homeland leaders, opposition politicians, everyone and anyone with a stake in the future of the country, and with a point of view on how that future should be decided. And that pattern of reporting has characterized most of what we see and hear in this country about the situation in South Africa.

What impressed me, and makes the situation in South Africa very different from that in other parts of the continent which have gone through the national dialogue about moving to a more representative form of government, is the belief among all the black leaders I met, that conditions must be created for the evolution of a system in which all South Africans, black and white, should be fully represented.

No one talked about pushing the 'white man' into the sea: there was a ready acknowledgement of the fact that white South Africans must have a place in any new society which emerges as a result of any future political reform. I found that extremely heartening and personally very pleasing since I'm a profound believer in equality of opportunity among peoples. Now, how that's accomplished is the big question and to some extent that's the story we've all been covering in South Africa, but at least, I found that some of the promises gave one some reason for hope.

There were some differences among the people I spoke to, about whether in the circumstances that hopeful outcome is not just a distant pipe-dream. President Botha says apartheid cannot last and it must be changed. Black leaders, and organizations like the African National Congress, say they are not sure what he means by 'change'. Leaders of the front line States — like President Kenneth Kaunda — say the current formulae being talked about as 'change' aren't sufficiently radical to avert widespread violence and blood-shed.

To that the Government would argue that it can only do what is possible at any one time; it has right—wing opponents to contend with, those who feel that there should be not the slightest deviation from the old grand concept of apartheid, and that any talk of change is heresy and is dangerous. That's the debate, the controversy we've all been reporting on in South Africa.

I do not think that debate has been greatly assisted by the current emergency regulations in which there are fairly tough curbs on what can be reported. In this country we would, as journalists, not relish the thought of receiving all our information in the form of 'hand-outs' from, say, the British Government's Central Office of Information. There's a great tradition of journalists finding out things for themselves and being able to report what they find out. All governments have an obvious interest in putting the best complexion on what they feel people should know or be told. In this country we have just gone through another tranche of disclosures about what really happened during the Suez crisis thirty years ago. The thirst of independent confirmation here is enormous. It probably isn't very different in South Africa, and when there is, as in that country, a majority of the population which feels that its voice is not being heard, then the consequences could be extremely serious.

Trevor McDonald
London, 1987

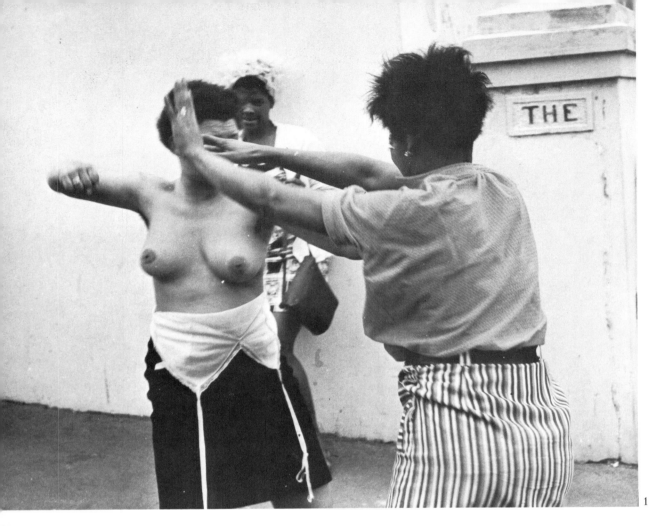

1,2. Two Coloured women fight it out over a man in the suburb of Tamboerskloof, Cape Town, 1969.

3. Coloured fishermen, Snoeklokermen, from a boat off Camps Bay, Cape Town, 1973.

4,5. Black squatter camp destroyed by the Stellenbosch Divisional Council in the Kraaifontein area near Cape Town, 1977. The camp was called the Jabulani camp, and these two photographs show one woman's shack. The first photograph is of the Divisional Council Workers removing her furniture, and the second photograph is of her watching with her neighbour while the bulldozer flattens her shack.

1

2

3

4

5

6

7

6. White anti-riot policeman beats Coloured child protester in the Athlone area of Cape Town during the 1976 rioting.

7. Police escort old woman past protesting demonstration by University of Cape Town students. St George's Cathedral, Cape Town, 1972.

8

8. Police and students of the
University of Cape Town clash
on campus, 1972.

9. South African
actor and baboon photographed
in Johannesburg 1978.

9

10. Miss South Africa (Andrea
Steltzer) visits children in the
Natalspruit Hospital, Germiston,
Johannesburg, to hand out
Christmas gifts, 1985.

11. White businessman, 'Kat' de
Beer, makes friends with
Alexandra township children
who stoned his factory. 1985.

12. Unwanted cats are put down
by the Booysens SPCA.
Johannesburg, 1986.

13. A pensioner looking lovingly
at his dog. Johannesburg. 1985.

12

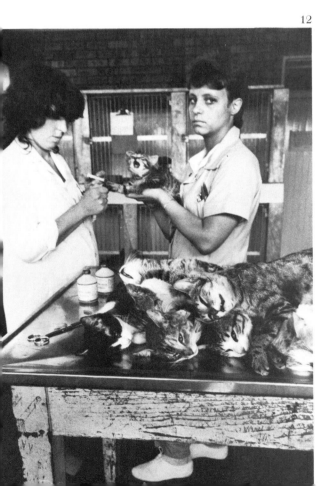

13

14

15

14,15. Funeral of Henry
Myandco who died on 7.1.87.
Van Jaarsveld Farm. Blinkport.

16,17. Clive Cupido, a Coloured
youth shot dead by police, lies in
his coffin at the local school
where a memorial service was
held for him. The first
photograph shows Clive's
grandmother greeting his
fellow-pupils. The second shows
Clive Cupido's family crying at
his graveside. These
photographs were taken in Cape
Town, 1985.

16

17

18–25. Police break up the planned march on Pollsmoor Prison by supporters of the Rev. Allan Boesak to demand the release of gaoled ANC leader Nelson Mandela in the Coloured area of Athlone, Cape Town, 1985.

18

19

20

21

22

23

24

25

26. Riot police chase black youngster in the Guguletu township near Cape Town, 1976.

27,28. Protesters and riot police
in action. Cape Town.

29. An armoured personnel carrier under attack in Cape Town.

30. South African Security Guard Association's annual pistol combat shooting championships held at a shooting range near Johannesburg, 1986.

31. Riot police beat a protester in the black township of Guguletu, near Cape Town. 1976.

32–34. Children at Coronationville, a Coloured township west of Johannesburg, play a game of 'policeman and freedom fighter'.

35. Coloured protesters
jeer army convoys patrolling the
streets of Athlone, Cape Town,
1985.

36. A black pickpocket is put to
flight by an angry crowd in
Market Street, Johannesburg,
1985.

37–42. During a riot in De
Villiers Street, Johannesburg, in
1985, pensioner Mrs Jane
Austen is attacked by rampaging
black youths and thrown to the
ground. While still prone, she is
robbed by other passing blacks.

37

40

38

41

39

42

43. Police beat a rioter with batons and
sjamboks during a riot in the
Cape Town city centre, 1985.

44. Protest at the University of the Witwatersrand (WITS) over the arrest of poet Breyten Breytenbach. Right-and left-wing students clashed: here we have a right-wing and a left-wing student fighting while other students look on.

45. New Year's Eve celebrations in Cape Town, 1974. Two Coloured men fight it out while police move in to break up the trouble.

46. Audience refreshments at a
Country and Western get-
together. Yeoville,
Johannesburg, 1983.

47. Children pose for the
camera: Hillbrow,
Johannesburg, 1986.

48–53. White hoboes in the
suburb of Yeoville,
Johannesburg, 1983.

50

51

52

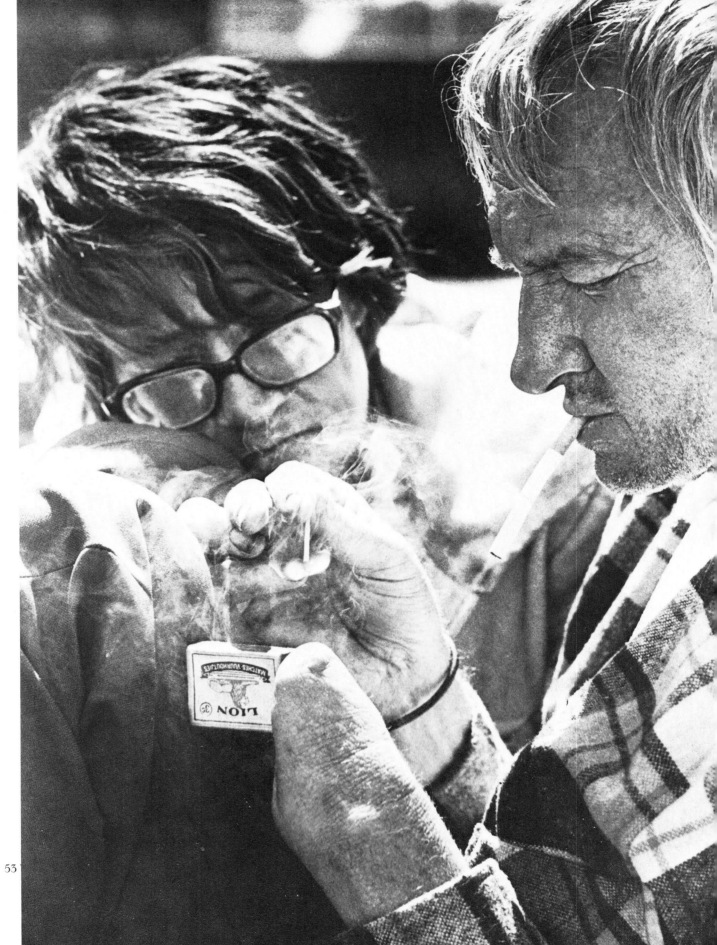

53

54,55. South African police
arrest University of Cape Town
students at the St George's
Street Cathedral, Cape Town,
1972.

56. Three policemen arrest woman University of Cape Town student at the St George's Street Cathedral, 1972.

57. While one policeman holds a box with sawdust and old-fashioned teargas bombs, a police sergeant grabs for one to throw at protesting students. Wale Street, Cape Town, 1972.

56

57

58. Police lieutenant pulls the hair of a protesting Cape Town student.

59. Policeman pushes woman student down a flight of stairs during troubles on campus, University of Cape Town, 1972. Another student tries to grab her from the police. In the background a policeman threatens a lecturer.

59

60. Rioter (or bystander?) shot by police in Athlone, a Coloured township near Cape Town, 1976. He is helped by other bystanders.

61. White policeman grabs a Coloured who moved into the exclusive whites only area at a pop festival held at the Greenpoint Stadium, Cape Town, 1972.

60

61

62

63

Support the mayoral fund

A SOUND MIND IN A HEALTHY BODY

By contributing no matter how small or large an amount to the Mayoral Fund,
c/o The Office of the Mayor.
9, Johannesburg.

62. Pensioners laughing and smiling at the Beehive Community Centre, Johannesburg, 1980.

63. Pensioner or hobo in a Johannesburg bus shelter, 1971. The man looks very tatty, and not at all well. The motif on the background is a mayoral plea: 'A sound mind in a healthy body'.

64. Pensioner, Johannesburg, 1983.

64

65. The Fairest Cape, 1985.

66

67

66,67. Suicide attempt by
Vincent Van Heerden, who
jumped from the YMCA
building, Long Street, Cape
Town, 1977. Vincent survived.

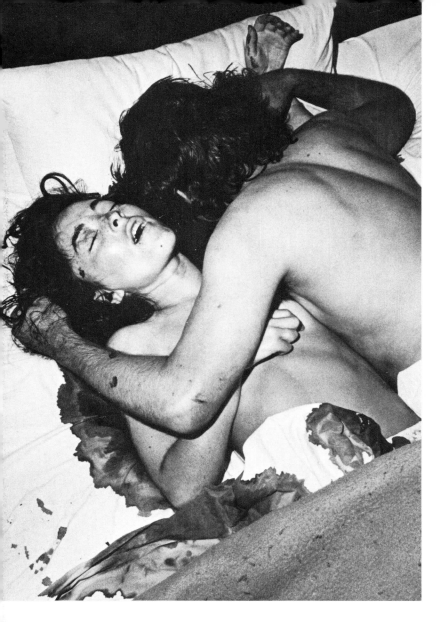

68. Murder/suicide, Cape Town, 1974. She was nineteen and divorced, he was thirty-three and also divorced. Both had children. They were going to get married but she said no. After a bout of drinking they went to bed, and while she was sleeping he shot her through the head and then himself. He still has the gun in his hand.

69. Dead ANC fighter in the Volkskas Bank, Silverton, 1980. He had been shot dead by the police.

70

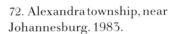

72. Alexandra township, near Johannesburg. 1983.

71

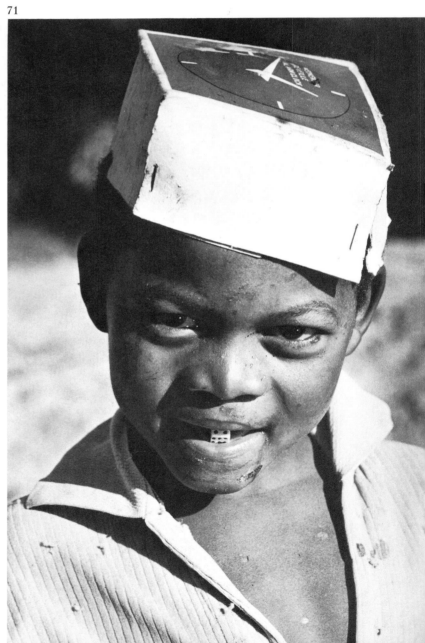

70. Man with dog in box. Johannesburg, 1980.

71. A child plays with a cardboard box and a dice. Johannesburg.

72

73,74. Soccer violence at the
Rand Stadium, Johannesburg,
during a match between
Hellenic and Kaizer Chiefs,
1974.

73

74

75,76. Soccer crowd at the Rand
Stadium, Johannesburg, 1979.

76

75

77–84. Police and soccer fans clash at a Cup Final match between Lusitano and Kaizer Chiefs at the Rand Stadium, Johannesburg, 1978.

77

78

79

80

81

82

83

84

85. White combatants at the Wynberg Rivonia Shooting Club, Johannesburg, 1985.

86. Police arrest white protesters at the St George's Street Cathedral, Cape Town, 1972.

87. Policeman throws tear-gas bomb (the old-fashioned glass type) at demonstrators in Wale Street, Cape Town, 1972.

86

87

88. Personal weaponry.

89. Black child with lollipop and traditional face-painting, Transkei Independence Celebrations, 1976.

90. Homeless black children clowning around for the camera in Hillbrow, Johannesburg, 1986.

91. Black child begs from white motorist, Hillbrow, Johannesburg, 1986.

92. Black child eats rotten bananas from a rubbish bin in Cape Town's Grand Parade market-place. 1970.

93

93. A Border farmer relaxes with his family and friends, near the Limpopo River, Northern Transvaal, 1985. (Note the gun in case of an emergency.)

94. Dwarf wrestlers at Portuguese Hall, Johannesburg, 1986.

95. White Johannesburg traffic policemen clown around with a gun and sunglasses for the camera. Johannesburg, 1974.

94

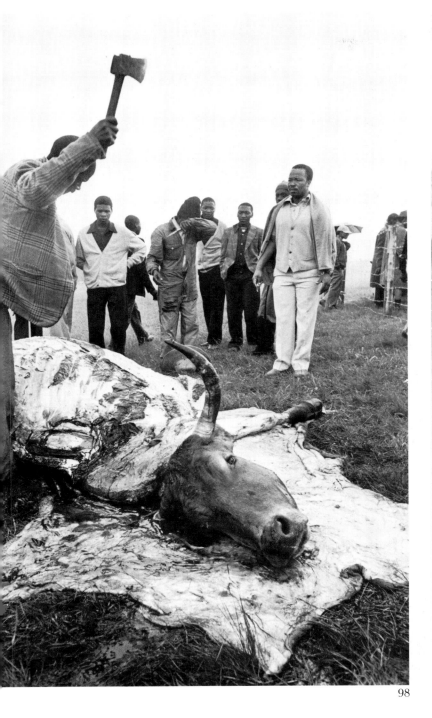

96. Black looter is shot by police with birdshot in central Johannesburg during a 1985 riot. He is then arrested.

97. The Press threatened by a plainclothes policeman, central Johannesburg. Note the whip in his hand.

98. Transkei Homeland Independence, 1976. Blacks slaughter an ox as part of celebrations.

99. Also Transkei Independence celebrations. Black man kills ox with penknife, 1976.

100,101. Mud-wrestling at a Johannesburg hotel, 1982. Shortly after this scene was photographed, mud-wrestling was banned by the Wrestling Control Board as indecorous.

102,103. By-election meeting held by National Party in the Louis Trichardt, Northern Transvaal. The first picture is of P.W. Botha and his wife arriving at the meeting, and the second is of a Nationalist child applauding. 1983.

104. Press conference by
Archbishop Desmond Tutu,
Johannesburg, 1985, calling for
an end to violence.

105. A lesson in self-defence

106. White hostages of the Silverton bank siege after being released by police. They were held by ANC 'fighters' (for want of a better word) after police opened fire. 1980.

110. New Year's Eve celebrations, Hillbrow, Johannesburg, 1979. A woman, (still smiling!) is bitten by a police dog.

111. New Year's Eve, Johannesburg , 1979. Man making an obscene sign.

108

109

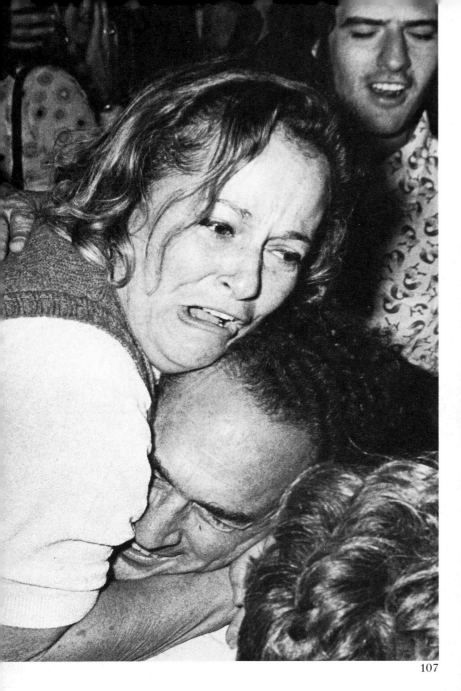

107

107. Supporters of Progressive Federal Party candidate Colin Eglin weep with joy after he won the Sea Point constituency in the 1974 General Election.

108. New Year's Eve celebrations, Hillbrow, Johannesburg 1979. A man squirts another man with a bottle of Coca Cola.

109. New Year's Eve celebrations, Johannesburg. A drunk with policeman, both white.

110

111

112

112. New Year's Eve, Hillbrow,
Johannesburg, 1979. People
hold hands to eyes after police
use tear-gas to disperse crowd.

113–115. Policeman who
ventured into a side street on his
own is attacked by a mob on
New Year's Eve. Johannesburg,
1979.

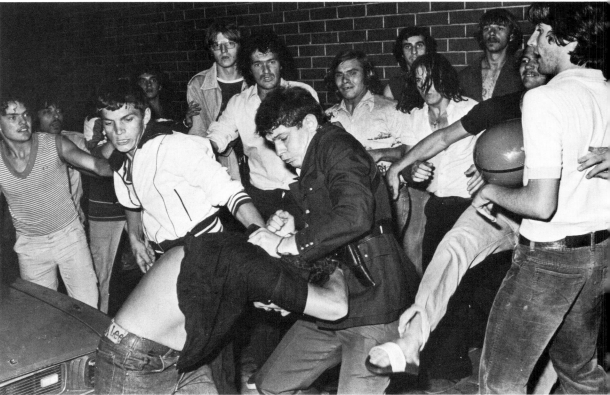

113

114

115

116

118,119. Railway police and
South African police
amalgamate at a parade at
Kempton Park, near
Johannesburg, 1986. The first
picture shows a white officer in
control of blacks; the second a
policeman on parade who
fainted due to the heat.

116. Black looter shot by police
during a riot, 1985. De Villiers
Street, Johannesburg.

117. A white self-protection
group have a get-together at a
gun club near Pretoria, 1980.

117

118

119

120,121. Whites with guns at a
shooting-range near Pretoria,
1980.

122

123

122. White Air Force recruits play with dummy of corporal in camp bungalow, 1973.

123. Members of the Citizens Band Radio Club Association hold a get-together and morning barbecue at a local supermarket. Johannesburg, 1978.

124. Target practice.

124

125

126

125–127. A Coloured woman beats her drunken husband with a stick. Cape Town, 1978.

127

128

128,129. Dagga–smokers:
Coloureds having a good old
lunchtime puff in an abandoned
building near Cape Town, 1975.
(Dagga is more commonly known
as cannabis.)

130. Bare-breasted Transkei
woman at Independence
celebrations, 1976.

129

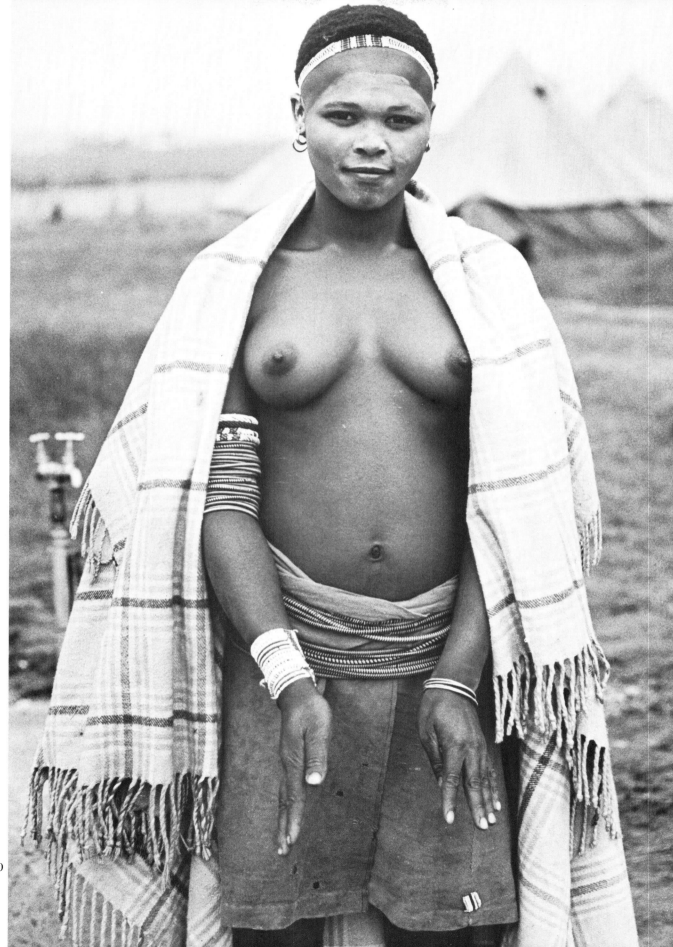

130

131

131,132. Window-dresser's dummy in bag at the Oriental Plaza, an Indian shopping complex, in Johannesburg, 1985.

133,134. Hillbrow, Johannesburg, 1985. Disabled black woman begs in street.

132

133

134

135. Drunken white man lies in
Hillbrow gutter, Johannesburg,
1985.

136. White pensioner begs from
passing blacks in the affluent
white northern suburb of
Randburg, Johannesburg, 1985.

137. Gladys Lee, South Africa's oldest and probably most famous protester, always inveighing against the Government and apartheid. Cape Town, 1972.

138. Homeless black child sleeps on pavement in morning sun, Hillbrow, Johannesburg, 1985.

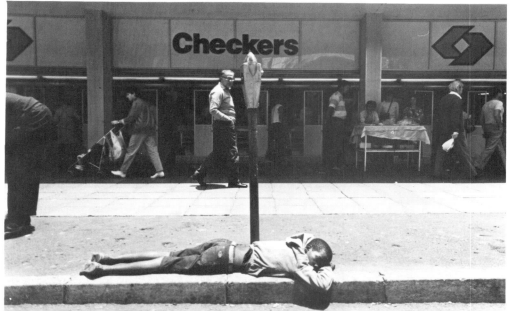

139. PLO anti-Jewish demonstration at the University of the Witwatersrand, Johannesburg, 1982.

140. Left-wing students at the University of the Witwatersrand tear up the South African flag, 1981.

141. Black WITS student shouts anti-apartheid slogans at a rally at the University in 1981.

140

141

142. 1984 engagement party of an ex-Miss Europe to local Johannesburg socialite Colin Sturgeon at a Johannesburg night spot.

143. A woman hides her face from the camera.

144. Mozambique, 1971.
Streetside photographer with
boy posing for his photograph.

145. Gangster, Malay Quarter, Cape Town, 1972. (I was on a rooftop photographing Coloured children when I suddenly heard someone shout, 'Whitey, take my photograph', and there was this man with a gun in the alley below. Terrified, I took one photograph. Satisfied, the man disappeared as quickly as he had arrived.)

146,147. Children peering under
a door and a man looking in a
window in the Malay Quarter,
Cape Town, 1972.

146

147

148,149. A Coloured child gets
dressed by her sister prior to being photographed — and poses for
the camera.

149

150

151

150. Railway police arrest a
black protester, Johannesburg Railway
Station, 1985.

151. Policeman arrests Coloured
pupils at a Cape Town school, 1985. The
school is the Vista High School for Coloured
children.

152. Coloured child playing with a roll of toilet paper, Malay Quarter, Cape Town, 1972.

153. Coloured child sitting in corner of a wrecked building.

152

153

154

155

154. Two Coloured people with
child and dog pose for camera.
Malay Quarter, Cape Town,
1973.

155. Coloured child urinating in
the street in the Malay Quarter.
Cape Town, 1973.

156. Coloured group, Malay Quarter, 1973

157. Man and wife after fight. Cape Town, 1973.

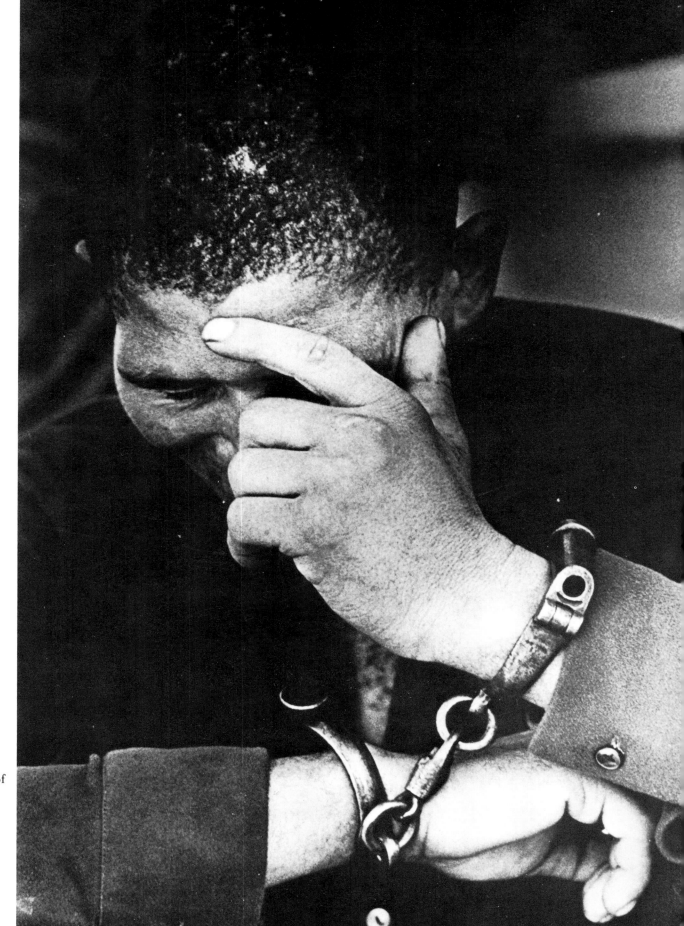

158. Coloured man accused of murdering white farming couple, is taken to the scene of the crime in handcuffs. (Early seventies.)

159. Riot policemen drag man
they shot away from township
crowd, 1976.

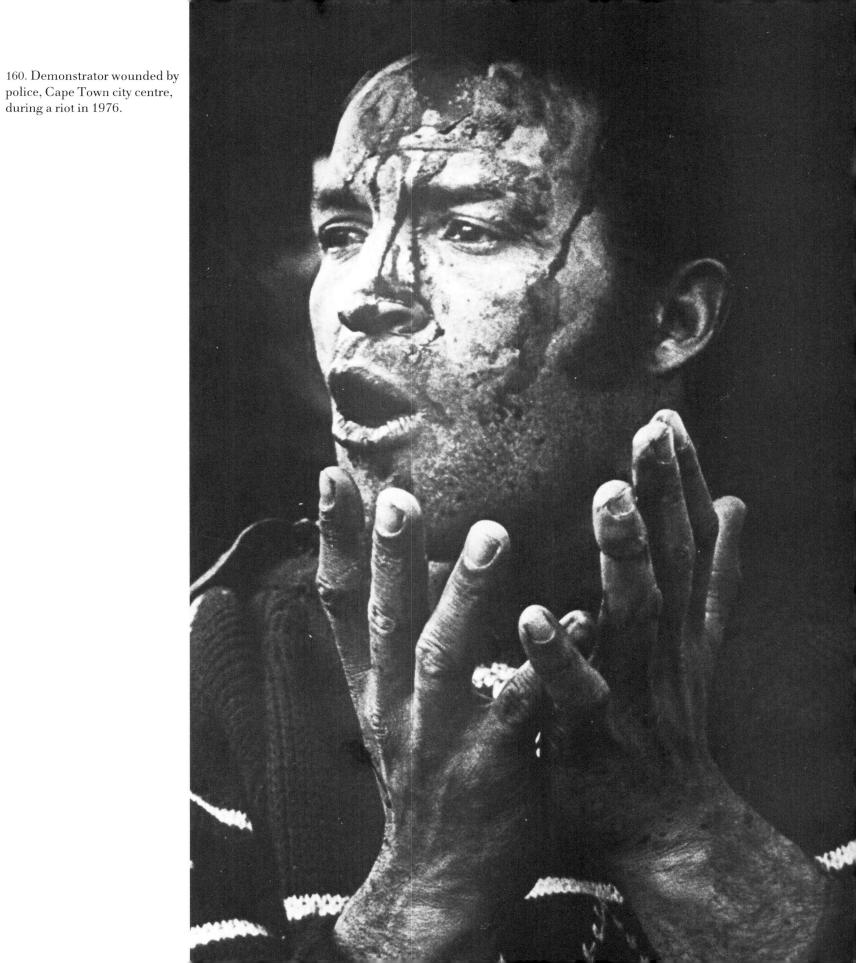

160. Demonstrator wounded by police, Cape Town city centre, during a riot in 1976.

161. Down-and-out people
sleep in open, District 6, Cape
Town, 1972.

162. Man and his dog, District 6, Cape Town, 1972.

163. Man and wife fight in Malay Quarter, Cape Town, 1976.

164. Coloured child, with arm in sling, poses for camera. Malay Quarter, Cape Town, 1973.

165. Three children pose for a photograph in street. Malay Quarter, Cape Town, 1973.

164

165

166. Children play in District 6,
Cape Town. Early seventies.

167. Coloured children play on
sand-dunes at Hout Bay, near
Cape Town, 1977.

168,169. Down-and-out Coloureds
who live in the mountains near
Cape Town scavenge in rubbish
bins and pose for the camera.
1976.

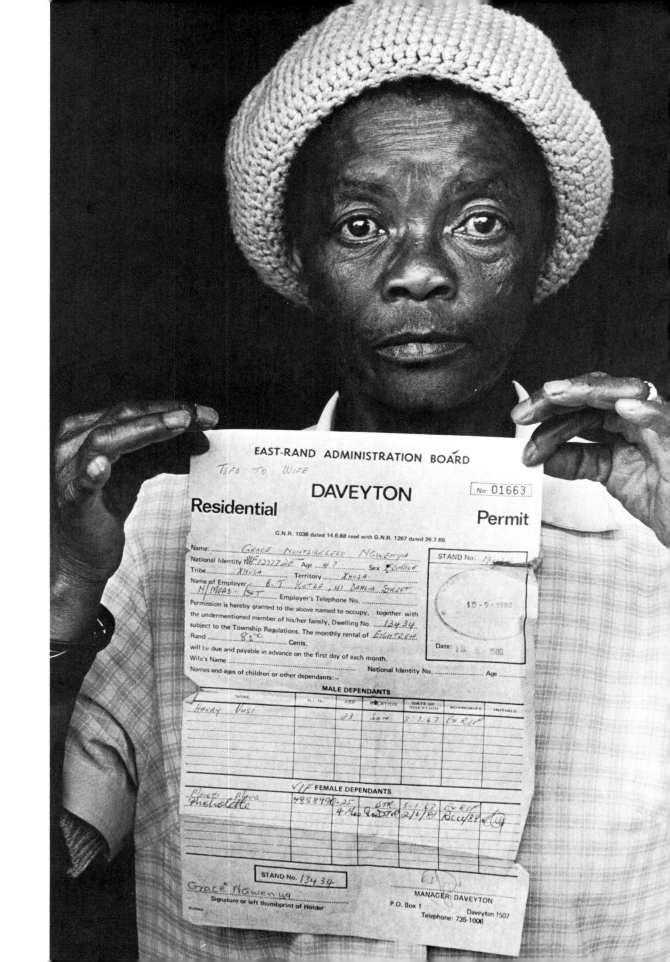

170. Black woman holds up her permit which allows her to stay in the black area of Daveyton, near Johannesburg. 1982.

171

171. Down-and-outs in Cape Town, 1976.

172. A Coloured down-and-out woman, in Cape Town, 1976.

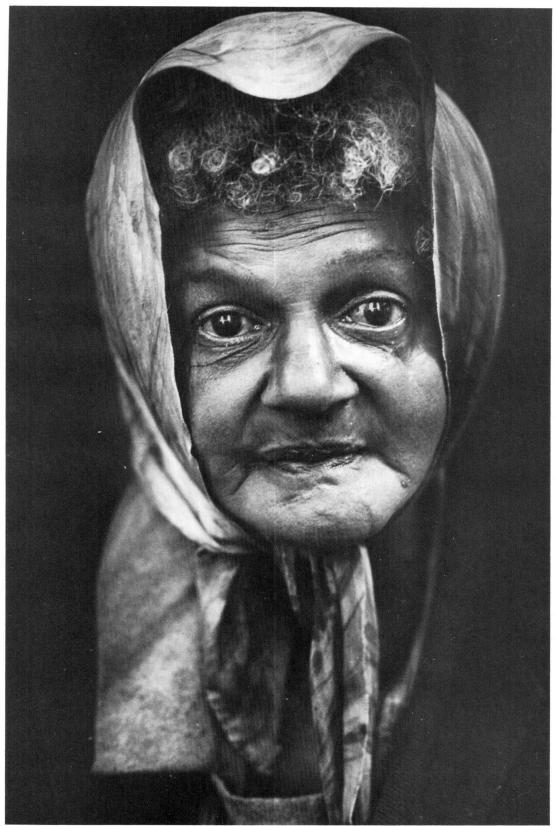

173–175. Beggar with mouth organ. Cape Town, 1971.

176. A Coloured beggar with the South African flag. Cape Town, 1971.

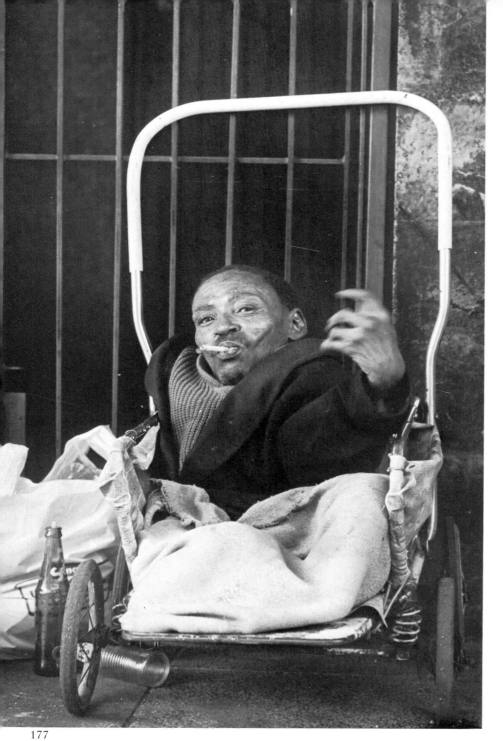

177

178

177. Beggar in pram with cooling bottle next to it, beckoning, cigarette in mouth. Johannesburg, 1976.

178. White farmer in the province of the Orange Free State shows part of his failed crop, ruined by the drought. 1984.

179. Down-and-out black man
in Johannesburg, 1975.

180. Federal Hotel,
Johannesburg, 1985. Three of
the locals with Mafia-type hats.

181. Brothel, New Doornfontein,
Johannesburg, raided by police
Vice Squad, 1984.

181

182. Johannesburg, 1979. Black
nanny with two white children
hits man on head with rock
because he made an improper
suggestion to her.

183. Student procession, WITS,
Johannesburg, to raise funds for
charity. 1982.

184. Refugee camp for Lesotho
refugees, Bethlehem, Orange
Free State, 1979. Naked black
child, hands behind back, walks
after mother.

182

183

184

185. Close-up of Uys Krige, famous South African poet. Photograph taken near Cape Town, 1974.

186. A landlady pensioner armed with gun, Johannesburg, 1983.

187. Boer War pensioner. Transvaal, 1982.

185

186

187

188. Young white male
prostitutes wait to be processed
at John Vorster Square police
station after being arrested by
the Vice Squad. 1984.

189. South African police
fingerprint procedure.
Johannesburg, John Vorster
Square, 1984.

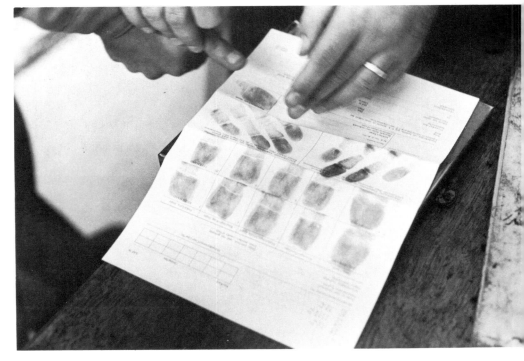

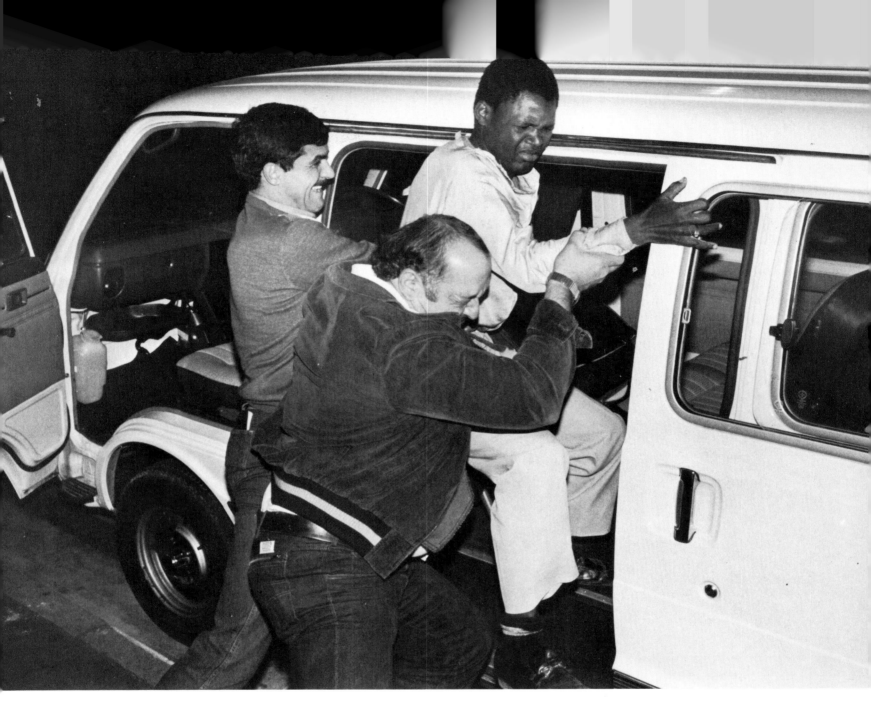

190. Male black prostitute is
arrested by police Vice Squad,
Johannesburg, 1984.

191. The pop festival in Johannesburg, 1975. People dancing and drinking.

192. Pop festival, Johannesburg, 1975. Fight in crowd.

191

192

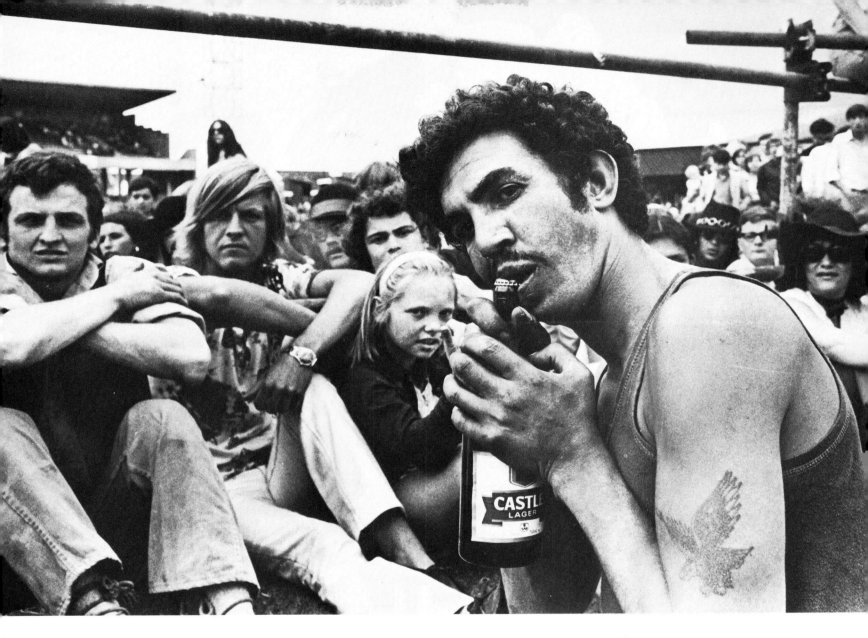

193. Pop festival, at the Hartley Vale soccer ground, Cape Town, in the early seventies. Man opens bottle of beer with his teeth.

194. A couple kissing at the Johannesburg pop festival, 1975.

195. Child labour in Botswana. Youth, 15 years old, lifts 100-kilogram bag of fertilizer destined for Zambia at a depot near Francistown, Botswana, 1978.

196. Armed border farmers, man and wife, with shotgun and pistol in holster. South Africa/Zimbabwe border, Northern Transvaal, 1985.

196

197. A cat out for early-morning walk, in District 6, Cape Town, 1972.

198. A shop dummy, in District
6, Cape Town. 1973.

199. District 6, Cape Town, 1973.

200. District 6, Cape Town. Man
and woman with baby plead to
be photographed.

201. The same: close up of man
with two pet dogs.

202. Children play in a truck, in District 6, Cape Town, 1974.

203. A child crying in District 6, Cape Town, 1974.

204. Group of children, Malay
Quarter, Cape Town, 1974.

205. District 6, Cape Town,
1974: man in shadows.

206. Malay Quarter, Cape Town, 1974. Dagga-smokers molest down-and-out sleeping in open lot.

207. Man silhouetted between pillars. Cape Town, 1974.

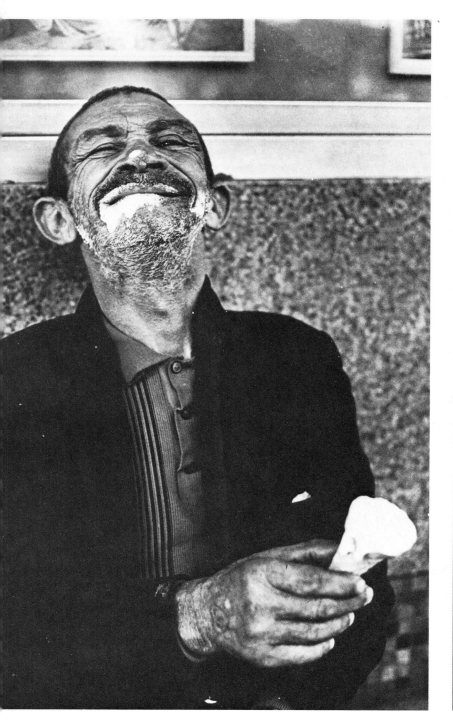

208,209. Saturday morning
drunk with ice cream cone. Cape
Town, early seventies.

210. Cape Town: children sliding down walkway in District 6.

211. Children looking in a shop window. District 6, Cape Town, 1974.

212. Angola, 1975. Refugee child
on Barracuda Beach, Luanda,
with outsized jacket.

213. Angola, MPLA troops on
back of truck with child carrying
a home-made gun.

214,215. Angola, 1975, Luanda.
Corpses found in drains after
MPLA won the battle for
Luanda.

216. An accident, in Johannesburg, in 1978. A man on a delivery motorcycle has crashed, and lies in road, surrounded by spectators.

217,218. Villiersdorp bus smash,
Cape Province, 1972. Bus
carrying a Coloured rugby team
and supporters back to Caledon
has crashed into river, with no
survivors.

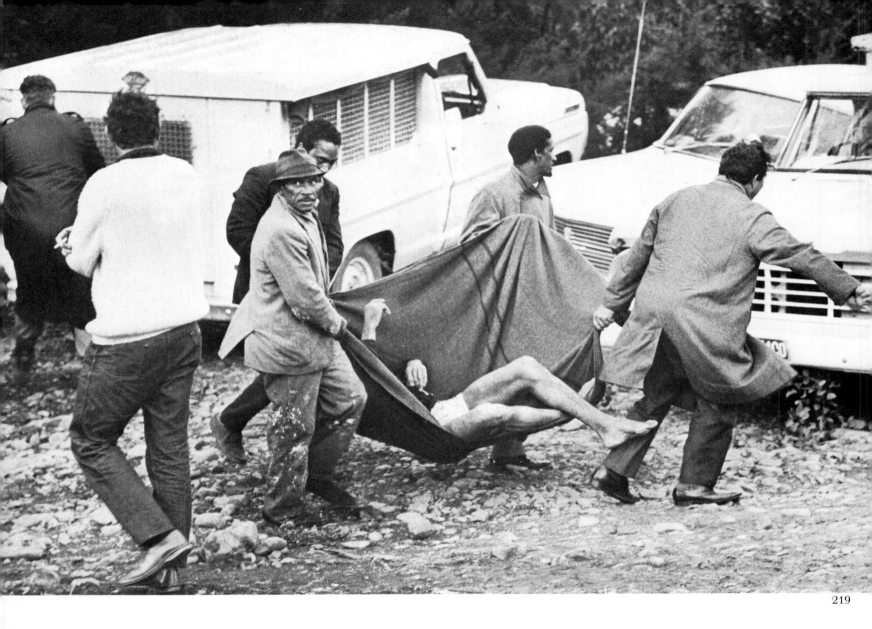

219,220. Bus smash, Villiersdorp,
fifty miles from Cape Town. The
first photograph shows the body
being retrieved, the second the
family at the graveside.

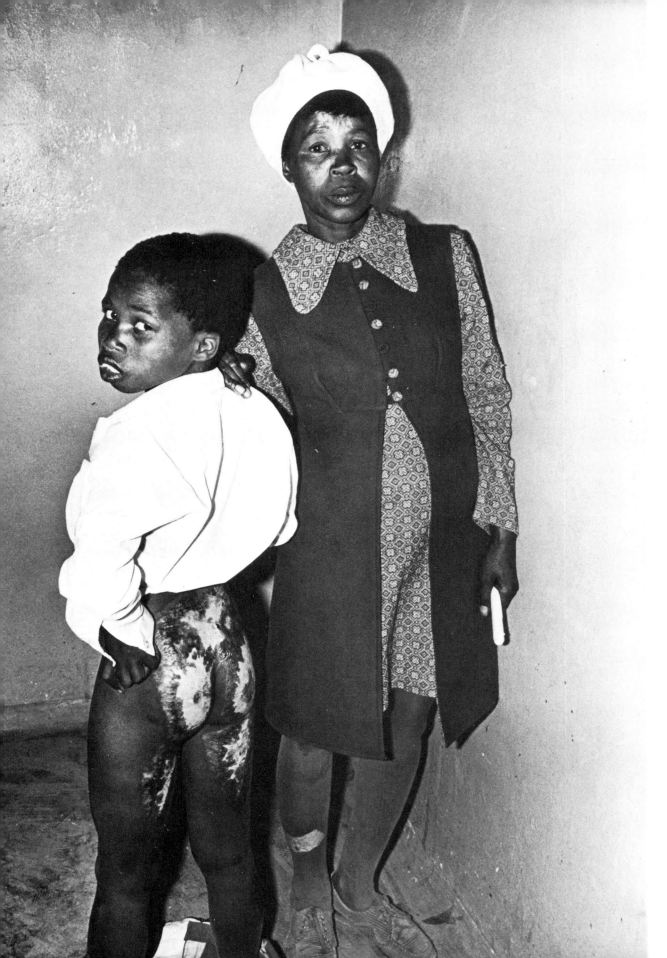

221. White railway train drivers assaulted this black child by sticking his buttocks into the open furnace of their locomotive. His crime: picking up coal alongside the railway tracks. 1974. Beaufort West, Cape Province.

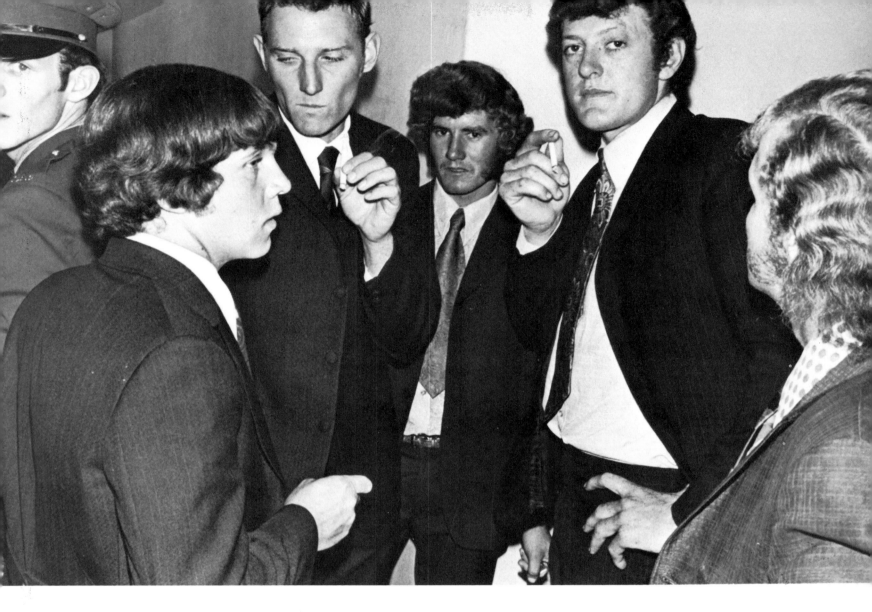

222. Some of the accused at the
trial at Beaufort West, 1974.

223,224. Accident unit, Groote
Schuur Hospital, Cape Town.
An epileptic has fallen into the
fire, and his burns are tended by
a nurse. Early seventies.

223

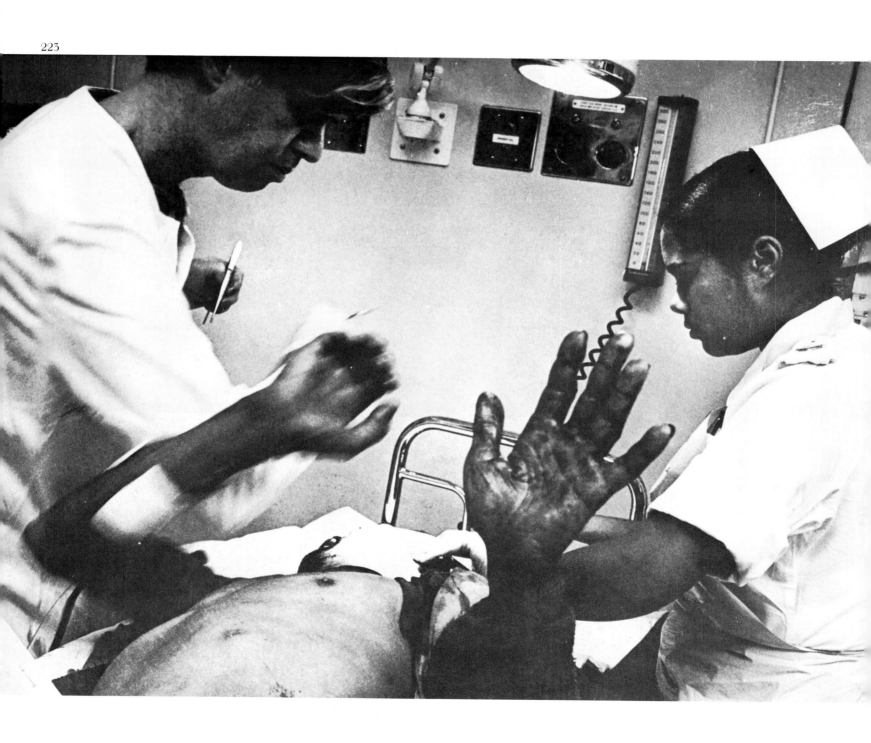

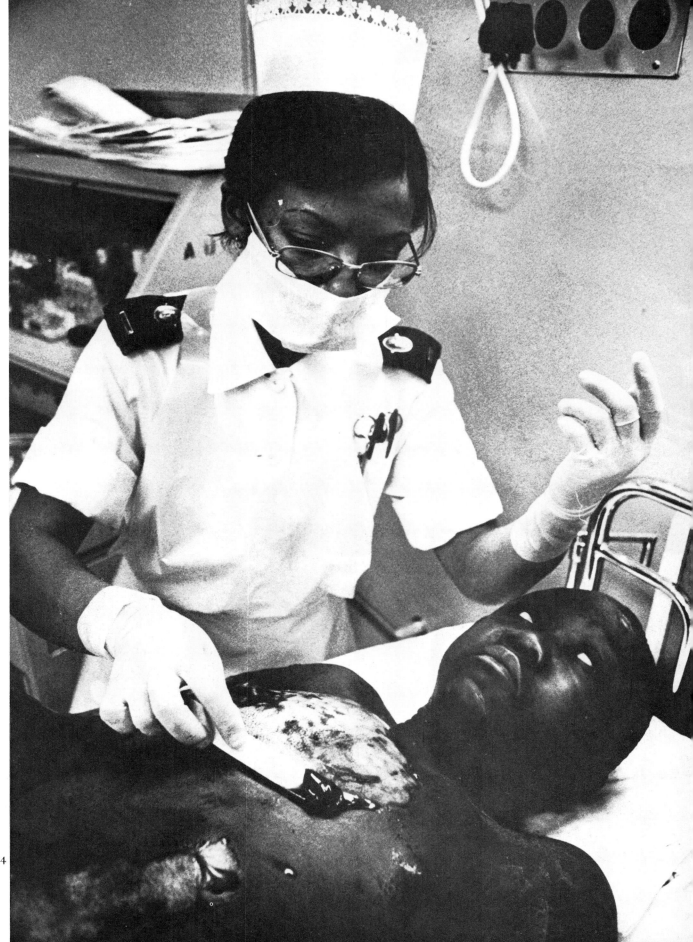

224

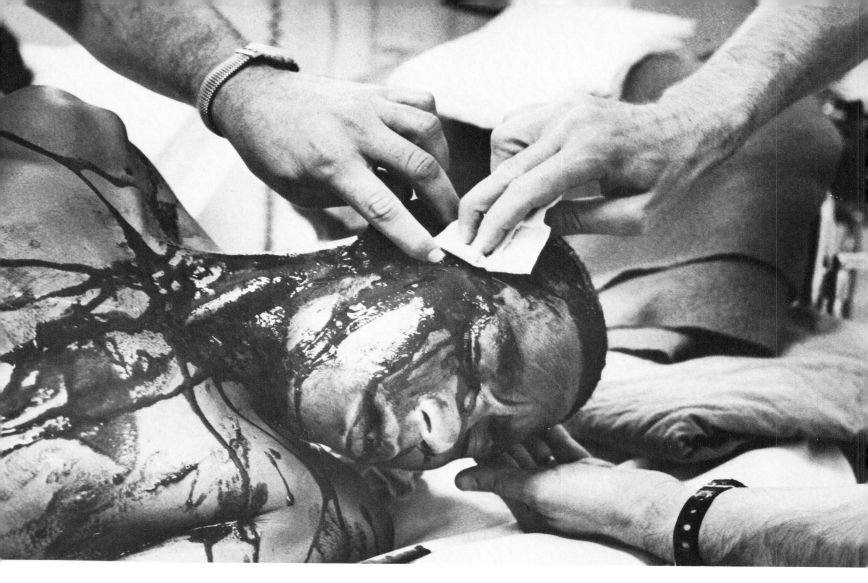

225. White doctor with his finger in the wound in a patient's head.

226. Accident unit, Groote Schuur Hospital, Cape Town.

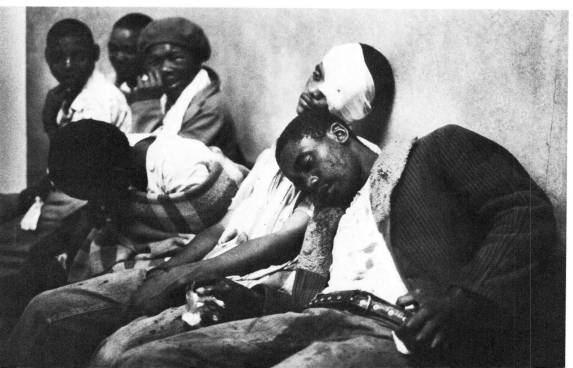

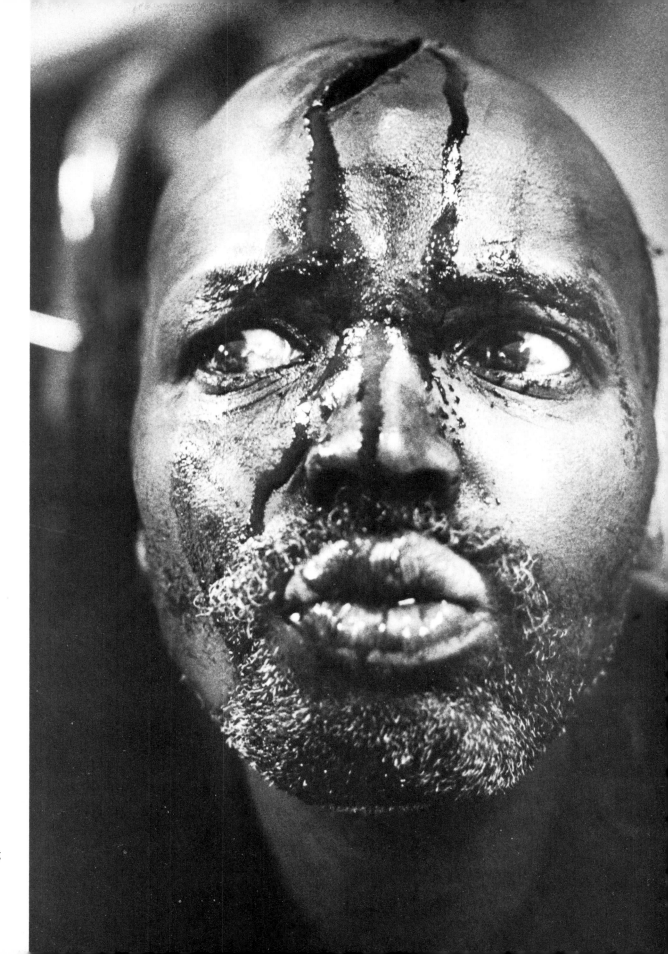

227. Close-up of a man bleeding
from a gash in his head.

228. Accident unit, Groote
Schuur Hospital, Cape Town.

229. Blacks wait at bus-stop near
Pretoria. Destination:
Stinkwater. 1975.

230. An accident, in Cape Town, involving a paint truck. Man covered in paint but otherwise uninjured. 1976.

231. FNLA/Unita refugees. Barracuda Beach, Luanda, Angola, 1975. Black woman with fish.

232. FNLA/Unita refugee washes her children in front of Palace of Justice, Luanda, after the fighting had stopped. Luanda, Angola, 1975.

231

232

233. Rhodesia, 1980.
Terrorist assembly
camp east of Salisbury.

234–236. Rhodesia, 1978.
Meeting in the Mondora
tribal trust land,
addressed by Bishop Abel
Muzorewa.

233

234

235

236

237. Local child welcomes
Frelimo solders after the war
ended in Mozambique, 1975.

238. Distracted by the
cameraman during drill at a
military parade.

239. White British subject, Larry
Bennett, living in South Africa,
with some of his weapons. 1980.

240. Rhodesia, 1978.
Soldier in Bishop Muzorewa's
private army.

241. Dancers at Transkei
Independence celebrations,
1976.

242. Upper class whites at clay
pigeon shoot, northern suburbs,
Johannesburg, 1986. They have
shotguns and champagne.

243

244

243. Inquest on Dr Neil Aggett, a political trade unionist who died at the hands of the police. Johannesburg Magistrates Court, 1982. Note the lone protester outside the court building.

244. Leader of AWB (Afrikaner resistance movement) Eugene Terre'Blanche tears up petitions for the opening of a Pretoria theatre to all races, 1978. The man on the extreme left of the photograph is a church minister who attacked and beat me after I took this photograph.

245. AWB leader Eugene Terre'Blanche arrives for a meeting in the Germiston suburb of Johannesburg, 1981. His stormtroopers are in the foreground, with the AWB eagle and 7 emblem on their back.

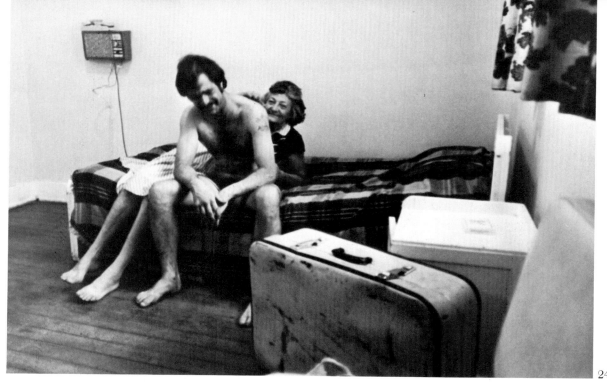

246. Down-and-out mother and son, Federal Hotel, Johannesburg. 1985.

247. Federal Hotel, Johannesburg, 1985. General pub scene.

248. Afrikaner resistance movement, (AWB) holds a meeting at Pretoria's Voortrekker monument in 1981. One man has a rifle, another holds a flag, and a child has a toy gun in his holster.

246

247

248

249

250

249–252. Poor whites,
Vrededorp, Johannesburg, 1980

251

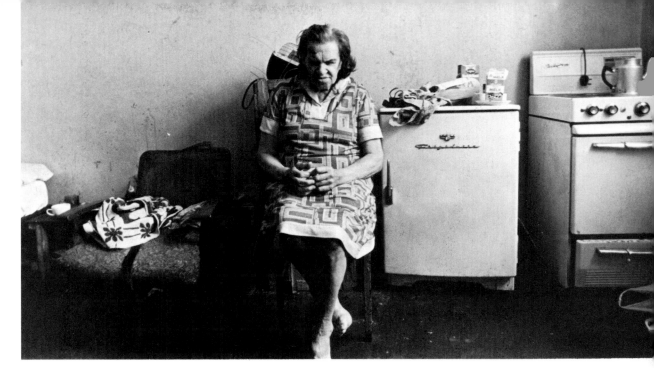

253,254. Pensioners,
Johannesburg. 1983.

255. Rhodesia, 1978. Memorial service in Salisbury for pilot of the passenger aircraft shot down by Nkomo terrorists. The wife of the pilot, Captain Hood, is led out of the church by the minister.

256. Blindfolded girls at an AWB picnic, near Johannesburg (northern suburbs), 1986.

257. Detained church leaders, 1980. They had marched in Johannesburg, and were arrested and held overnight at the Magistrates Court before being released.

258. Visit to Soweto by
Nationalist Minister Koornhof,
1980. Police keep angry crowd at
bay.

259. Blacks in crowd awaiting
Minister Koornhof's arrival
indicate what they think of him
and the Sowetan mayor. One
black has a rope around his
neck, while others are pulling at
it.

260. Banana seller, District 6,
Cape Town, early seventies.

261. Black squatters, Cape Flats,
near Cape Town. 1973.

262. Black clinic, Johannesburg
North. 1984. Close-up of black
baby cradled in white hands.

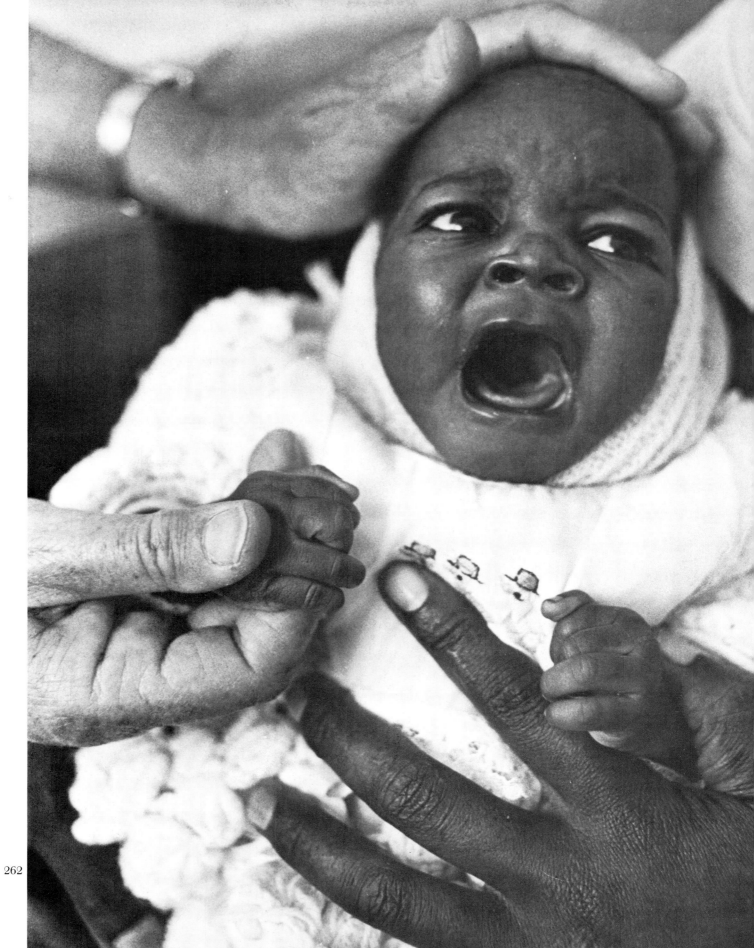

263,264. People allowed into drive-in cinema, Johannesburg, for the preview of the Walt Disney film *Aristocats*. They got in at half-price on condition they brought along their cats. 1979.

265. Film made in Cape Town, 1976, called *Dingetjie and Idi Amin* with actress Narina Ferriera ticketing a camel in Wale Street, Cape Town.

266. Male stripper at a hotel in Germiston, a suburb of Johannesburg. 1983.

265

266

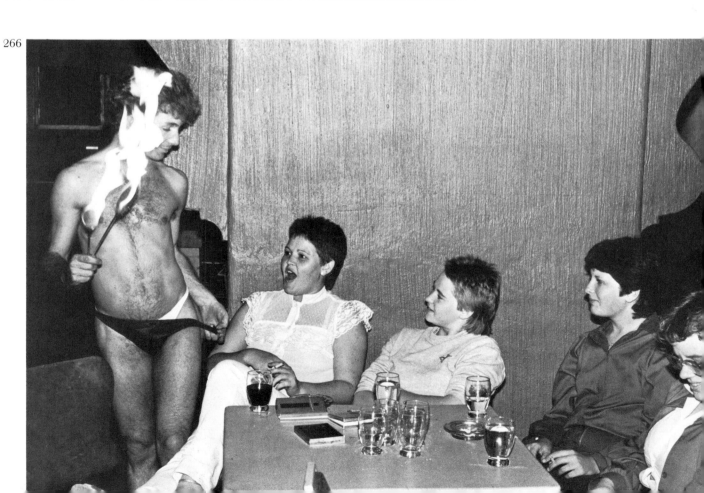

267,268. Fishermen, Hout Bay,
Cape Town. 1985.

267

268

269. Fish hawkers in Cape
Town, 1985.

269

270

271

272

270–272. Play *Death For Freedom* by black playwright Sebuya Miya, depicting the near necklacing to death of a black policeman by angry township residents.

273. Fight in the crowd at a rugby match, Cape Town, 1976.

274. AWB meeting, August 1986. Pretoria.

275. Children and grandmother,
Benoni, Johannesburg, 1986.

276. White border farmers in the
Northern Transvaal, 1985.